JAMES LEACH
Poems & Stories
Book 4

A book of poems and short stories for all ages offering a glimpse into the wild and crazy experiences of Kansas native James Leach

Also by James Leach

Wild Wanderings of a Worldly Mind

Jim with a live tiger in Moscow, Russia.

Available on Amazon.com in North America, Europe, and Great Britain.

Also by James Leach

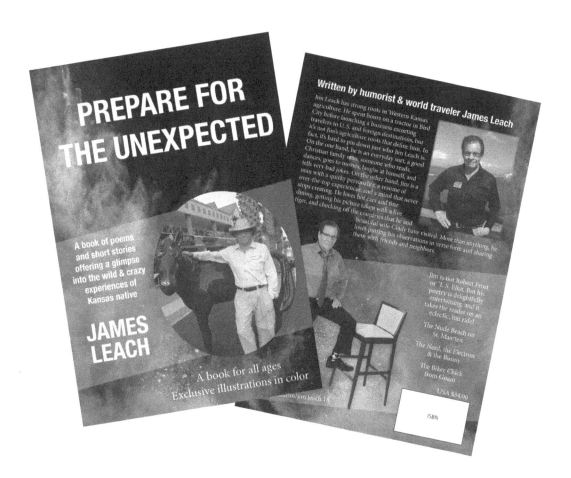

Prepare for the Unexpected

Available in color on Amazon.com
in North America, Europe,
and Great Britain.

Also by James Leach

(exceptionally extraordinary)
OUT OF THE BOX

A book of poems and short stories offering a glimpse into the wild and crazy experiences of Kansas native

JAMES LEACH

A book for all ages
Illustrated by 14 artists
Includes 223 personal photos
of his life and world travels

Out of the Box

Jim has driven this 2021 C-8 Midengine Corvette hardtop convertible 175 MPH. The Corvette factory lists the top speed at 196 MPH. The mural behind the Corvette is the Wichita city flag.

Jim's poetry is delightfully entertaining, and it takes the reader on an eclectic, fun ride!

Orphan Boy	Love on the Mississippi	The American Soldier
How Old is Grandpa?	The Dog & The Pig & The Pig's Brother	
Bottom Squirter	The Old Man and The Boy	Mach 2
A Surprise Blizzard	Poverty Street	The Curse of Beauty

James (Jim) Leach has strong roots in Western Kansas agriculture. He spent hours on a tractor in Bird City before launching a business escorting travelers to U. S. and 148 international destinations, but it's not Jim's agriculture roots that define him. In fact, it's hard to pin down just who Jim Leach is. On the one hand, he is an everyday sort, a good Christian family man, someone who reads, dances, goes to movies, laughs at himself, and tells very bad jokes. On the other hand, Jim is a man with a quirky personality, a resume of over-the-top experiences, and a mind that never stops creating. Jim wrote his first poem in the second grade. He loves hot cars and fine dining, getting his picture taken with a live tiger, and checking off the countries that he and beautiful wife Cindy have visited. More than anything, he likes putting his observations in verse form and sharing them with friends and neighbors.

facebook.com/jim.leach.16

Available on Amazon.com in North America, Europe, and Great Britain.

JAMES LEACH
POEMS & STORIES
BOOK 4

Dedicated to my parents, Ralph and Ruth Leach.

James Leach, a former farmer, has led an exhilarating, unusual lifestyle as an international traveler. He and his wife have escorted hundreds of eager sightseers to destinations around the world. Possessing a prolific and brilliant imagination, this book lays out master compilations of poetry, prose, and experiences to share with you.

Self-published through Kindle Direct Publishing
First Edition

Copyright April 6, 2023 by James Leach

Acknowledgements

Thank you to my wife Cindy, of 59 years (1964), for her spontaneous enthusiasm throughout my life! Cindy will book a tour for you: jctours.com

To Gianna Scott and Megan Stull of Flamingo Ink for their patience and diligence in assembling the book for production.

Table of Contents

Table of Contents

Thoughts

Thoughts are created exponentially on a global plain.
They travel at the speed of light and come from the human brain.

Eight billion individuals thinking thoughts throughout the day.
Mental pictures are happy, sad, euphoric or in disarray.

May the longitudes and latitudes of the world converge.
May the dreams of creators accelerate and surge.

Let's tear apart these thoughts that our children should not possess.
Let's build a tower of love, a gentle breeze will caress.

Life

From the birth canal, they come to the starting line.
The forecast is not ubiquitous by design.

Each individual begins the race of life.
Some will gather love. Others will be burdened with strife.

Ideas ricochet through continents of people.
Blasting their resolve from the highest steeple.

Wisdom accumulates through the tunnels of time.
Let's protect those we cherish from harm or crime.

The race ends for some, a satisfied lot.
Happiness is a hidden gem that can't be bought.

Let our positives outweigh the other side.
And our wishes on a dove's wing may glide.

Peace

The sun collides with the horizon to end the day.
Then the sky is consumed by darkness as I start to pray.

Are my requests for fame and fortune out of place?
Might I speak of gratitude for blessings that ground my base?

Let my focus concentrate on the many in need.
Heal the sick, feed the hungry, love the lonely. Subdue our greed.

As life on this planet evolves, let peace capture each heart.
May every individual among the billions take part.

From the Dark Water

From the fathoms of the ocean, a molecule survives.
She is alone, and through the dark water, she arrives.

Is the mystery of her existence concealed in space?
Is the safety for humanity there to embrace?

Might a wise man solve the molecular puzzle?
Is it the key to love like a puppy dogs nuzzle?

Are the thoughts we accumulate mired in negative doubt?
Or is it possible from the depths of the sea, kindness will sprout?

Lost

The small boy stands at the corner of Birch and Third Street.
The chocolate melts in his hand from the summer heat.

He looks for his mom as a tear creeps down his sunburned cheek.
A frantic mother stands with her legs trembling and weak.

"Officer, he's three years old and wears a blue plaid shirt!"
The police immediately sent out an amber alert.

Cell phones across the city are receiving the text.
The entire metropolitan police force seems perplexed.

The little boy has his puppy on a leash, and they are lost.
They chased a Monarch butterfly and Birch Street they crossed.

A lady notices the boy is sobbing, so she stops.
After kneeling beside the child, she quickly calls the cops.

"We'll find your mommy, honey; I'll stay with you until we do."
This future young man clings to the lady and murmurs, "Thank you."

The toy poodle senses something is wrong and licks the boy's face.
Both parents rush from the police car to the boy and embrace.

He is surrounded by joy and smothered in kisses.
The love of our children is among our riches.

Twinkle Little Star

The star, as she twinkles, looks at her surroundings.
Her nearby friends sparkle as they float on sprouted wings.

The heavens are awake with divine activity.
Handsome angels are displaying obvious chivalry.

The stars and the angels share common equality.
Surrounded by the universe, a magic actuality.

The angels and the stars protect the earth people.
It's a delicate balance as through the eye of a needle.

A child's worry and tears are encouraged to escape.
A father's concerns and frustrations might an angel reshape.

May our souls be captured by angels and the great one.
And can we believe eternity has just begun?

A Rumor

It's only a rumor. I don't believe it is true.
You can hear anything on the street. There's always something new.

A strange message: I have heard it from more than one place.
Some rumors turn into gossip. This might be the case.

I now believe the rumor. It arrived here at night.
A beautiful baby has been born. His name is Jesus Christ.

The Slow Lane

Driving in the slow lane is not that bad.
The competitive fast lane can turn out sad.

More money, more cars, more lavish clothing.
Your bank account, we are not disclosing.

Shall we slow down and collect other things?
Not jewelry, coveted by queens and kings.

In the time we have left, let's gather our friends.
Concentrate on love and the message it sends.

Centuries of Knowledge

Do we accumulate imaginations that predict the future?
Do we look back at Genghis Kahn as a supreme ruler?

Did the accomplishments of Attila the Hun warn us?
And may Socrates' wisdom multiply our thoughts as we fuss.

Should the centuries of knowledge enable us to survive?
Will the murky shadows of darkness among us thrive?

I command you, my brethren, to step up to a place and shine.
We can excel and conquer as if encouraged by the divine.

Let the foul smells of defiance disappear from the earth,
And may the babies of our children behold a new birth.

The Educated Badger

The badger is a lawyer. At times he is vicious.
His clients pay in cash, and his sharp teeth are audacious.

I am skeptical, but a business partner I do need.
I found badgers are intelligent. This impressed me, indeed.

I am being sued by a small brown-haired wealthy rodent.
His demeanor is sarcastic, and his odor is potent.

His wife is decked out in Fifth Avenue attire.
Her sizzling personality seems to be on fire.

You know, too much money can turn a person off.
The badger tells me, "Calm down; let's play a round of golf."

I pray to above, the foul language I'm holding back.
This lady rodent uses words my vocabulary does lack.

I will steer the helm and find our destination.
I avoid thinking of a rodent's castration.

Because of their money, they bit off more than they could chew.
We beat them in court. Who next will they try to screw?

Magic Liquid

Does the human heart exude love when it pumps the substance of the living?
Is this life-sustaining liquid an embodiment of our emotional giving?

Let our fragile sentiments travel through a maze of arteries and time.
Shall their journey meander out of the melancholy depths, and may they climb?

To a new horizon that parallels the magnification of love renewed.
And our steadfast commitment to our fellow beings will be unmoved.

My Friend

Can you or I create a new way to think?
Is an explosion in our mind on the brink?

Does the great emancipator release our brain?
From conventional thoughts that are boring and mundane?

Let's eliminate crime and war, and evil from the earth.
We will command our cerebral desires to a rebirth.

Cast out those demons that try to stand firm.
Slash their wrists and end their hateful term.

Let all the darkness stop and bring love to you and me.
I will hold your hands, and what great friends we will be.

The Old Man is Dying

The old man is dying. The family gathers around.
The young'uns barely know him. His wrinkles appear heaven bound.

A grandchild brings a puppy. The mood is changed somewhat.
His wife remembers the years when his white hair she would cut.

And what memories some have. Is it that important now?
Can his body rest in a grave? May this we allow.

In misery, he is, and his wish is for death.
Pneumonia and the flu, an old man's friend for his last breath.

Too Many Pills

Twenty-two pills I take, and this is once a day.
Confusing it is, but I do what the doctors say.

The colors are different, and the sizes are not the same.
A mix-up can happen, although this was not my aim.

My Tylenol and stool softener pills are the same size.
The side effects of this mistake caught me by complete surprise.

Not one stool softener, but two I accidentally did take.
After sitting on the toilet, it was hard to put on the brake!

Eliquis, a blood thinner, is designed to prevent a stroke.
Miss this pill and an emergency you're likely to provoke.

Up to fifty times their size, the fiber pills will expand.
Diverticulitis is the culprit at hand.

I believe two memory pills a day are helping me out.
For three years now, I remember more, without a doubt.

Purchase an antioxidant with some of your cash.
It's like buying car insurance to prepare for a crash.

Nasty germs are ubiquitous. They're ready to attack.
Antibiotics prepare for battle. Courage they do not lack.

Hurricane

It's a storm, a hurricane; It's heading our way.
Forecasts vary; shall we follow Europe or nay?

We've lived here forever, an experience we possess.
Florida is a puzzle; where it lands, we only guess.

The category is discussed, one to even five.
My loved ones are very close; I hope we all survive.

Regarding the global warming issue, arguments do prevail.
This enormous storm is moving at the pace of a snail.

Tampa, they say, may be a direct hit.
September and October, the fuse has been lit!

Preparations are made, and sandbags are packed full.
Drownings are prolific, and survival is doubtful.

The storm rears its obstinate head and decides to stay in the south.
Pay attention to her. She's a girl with a loudmouth.

But take heed, my darlings, and shelter in a nearby cave.
Way over a hundred deaths are destined for a lonely grave.

And the politicians, who are so fiercely in debate,
Are Americans who have turned to love from hate!

Let's pause on our knees and salute the great one.
And love our sisters and brothers as this day is done.

I View Earth, The Planet

As my sight focuses down, I view earth, the planet.
A man's tears splash on his son's tombstone staining the granite.

The oncologist's diagnosis creates sobs worldwide.
Will the miraculous advances in science turn the tide?

I see smiling children everywhere beginning their life.
Miles down the road, a trucker shares a trip with his wife.

The ice is melting; huge icebergs seek their route to the south.
Death Valley forecasts record highs and continued drouth.

Globetrotting, I see kangaroo babies in a comfy pouch.
A small girl in Asia experiences her first hot stove, "Ouch!"

Jungles on this sphere are prolific with unseen danger.
Flip the coin to Europe and meet a beautiful stranger.

Fire consumes gigantics of acres here and abroad.
Generous profuse rains surprise us, and we are awed.

Abundant weather tragedies confuse our decisions.
Caring neighbors emerge with life-saving provisions.

As we spin the bottle, let there be more good than bad.
Let's balance our observations and disguise our thoughts if sad.

The Baby Tree

The baby Ponderosa Pine observes the trees growing near him.
Dwarfing his size and confidence, his majestic future is grim.

The massive living and wooden monoliths humble all that surround them.
Baby Pine reflects with awe at the challenges his future holds for him.

The little tree's needles are hit by a sunbeam that comes through the foliage so dense.
This ray of light quickly boosts the tiny tree's attitude and breaks the suspense.

Might he someday become bigger, not grandeur, but at least average?
And let his determination be driven by unyielding courage.

Black Holes and Our Celestial Ball

The enormity of space blows the mind.
Yes, Einstein, the 4th dimension is entwined.

Comprehension is inconceivable.
Exciting new findings are believable.

Imagine a black hole four million times our sun.
A grain of sand, this speck called earth, has just begun.

Science finds space expands. Does it ever end?
Our brilliant, though tiny heads can't comprehend.

We each wonder, and our intellect is spaced out.
The avenues of thought expose our doubt.

Is there oxygen, or is there life out there?
A place we can live with an atmosphere?

Shout to Our Community

He says it's absurd and throws them in the litter box.
The homeless people in the tents are the ones he stalks.

It's a complicated world for folks who have nothing.
And did (not to fit in) capture them by bluffing?

Did the creators of their birth abandon the lot?
What shallow words can describe this pitiful thought?

Could insignificant me or you ponder a way to assist?
Might our mystery equivalent appear in a foggy mist?

And I scream, and I tremble to support these different people.
Are we also the ones that didn't fit in as an equal?

Have our friends begun to accept defecation on the street?
Will we lie down, roll over and admit to our own defeat?

Or should we shout out to our communities from the highest steeple?
And join arms to encircle these extraordinary people?

An Old Man Loves Football

The mundane life of an eighty-year-old is refreshed by American football.
I am inundated with traumatic feelings from this fun, competitive brawl.

My youth has fled, and I recall my inept ability at football in high school.
Our favorite football teams, we realize, can't practice on the field, the golden rule.

The hard knocks to these tough players' bodies are football at its best.
As an old man, I cringe as the young men tumble with unorganized zest.

Shoestring tackles don't always work because leaping ball carriers fly through the air.
The art of passing and receiving is the shortcut to a win and an answer to prayer.

American competitive sports have influenced the future of our country.
With the aggressive thinking of our football players, let our competition flee.

The Soldiers are Marching

The soldiers are marching and marching and marching.
Through millenniums of time, the data keeps knocking.

War is the culmination of disagreement.
Can the warring tribes reach for appeasement?

History can be nasty and discouraging.
Are our prayers disguised as begging?

Is it useless to ask for peace on earth?
Could soldiers of the world experience a new birth?

Ma-mah had been Sick

Ma-mah has been sick for much of the winter.
Our hopes for a cure begin to fray and then splinter.

The decades she did mentor come crashing into our thoughts.
We cherish the love and discipline as we connect the dots.

Is she really on that pedestal we hold so high?
Did she always comfort us when we felt we had to cry?

Did she protect us as a German Shepherd would?
Did her bark of defiance only project good?

Have we slacked off when more love we should be giving?
Does this lady we love set an example for living?

Since papa passed, she has been our one and only rock!
Is her end near as a hand passes the numbers on our clock?

When the final day arrives, our hearts melt with sadness.
Mixed emotions of love, regret, and confusion plague us.

A Sticky Steering Wheel

A sticky steering wheel is not my favorite thing.
My steering wheel is fancy and has some extra bling.

Please scrub your hands if you want to drive my auto.
Jelly or honey brings my spirits to a low.

If you like a sticky steering wheel, drive your own car.
And for my finicky self, stay away from me and far.

The Silent Observer

I'm a silent observer watching from a distance.
They want me to join, but I show them resistance.

I teeter, and I totter; who makes their rules?
Intelligent they are or utter fools.

May the binary switches flip on and off.
Their words are shallow; I pout, and I scoff.

Laced with magical trickery, it's a sales pitch.
Let the yays and nays decide. My mind will switch.

Curve Ball

My forehead is all wrinkled, and I know why.
I squinted my way through life, and it makes me cry.

My crow's feet extend to a length that is shocking.
I am scolded by the bird that is mocking.

No sunscreen, and now my skin I sacrifice.
With patches of cancer, I now pay the price.

An intricate puzzle life sends with a curve ball.
We discover too late that there is no recall.

Step Ahead

It started as a thought from I know not where,
Accompanied by a sound that seemed to clear the air.

The marriage of these two parts created a song.
These pleasant vibes suggest that all's right and nothing's wrong.

As the spring winds cleanse a muddled and confused mind,
May we step ahead and leave the bad behind.

Lost in a Mirage

It appeared as a mirage when I started to flee.
The recurring blur mesmerized my psyche.

Comprehension is beyond my timid reach.
Sounds from my ancestors as they firmly preach.

The rules are changing, and we anticipate peace.
But place caution before you. The pressures won't cease!

Mamma, I Miss You

Mamma, I miss you. The years have gone by.
I'm seeking laughter, and my tears won't cry.

When I picture your face, it shows a smile.
You would willfully walk the second mile.

I was a handful at times, and this I know.
But you taught me straight rules, as flies the crow.

I'm now the same age as you at your death.
I'll save you a hug when I breathe my last breath.

Enriched

The darkness consumes her forehead spreading down her body.
The sculptor's reckless cuts are unseemingly shoddy.

The precision allure of her legs is lost in rude behavior.
May the artist be rescued by a bountiful savior.

Can the brilliance of a sunrise change the texture of her skin?
And the music smooths her mind from the strings of a violin.

Let each sunbeam devour this lady and penetrate her pores,
And the beauty of her life is enriched by mine and yours.

A Peek at the World

She was newly born and peeked out from her nest.
To behold a world of beauty and zest.

A raindrop, a teardrop, the mysteries of life itself.
Her view is eloquent by an imagined elf.

What challenges await this feathery friend?
May her youthful aspirations set a new trend.

Let her first flight soar to lofty new places,
And the hand she holds, a Full House with Aces.

Leather Gloves Cover My Fists

The wind blows straight but is forced to maneuver around the branches of the trees.
We as humans strategize our pathway to a life we hope for at ease.

But might we aggress our thinking to render fierce remarks to some peers?
Let us defend our morals and see where this vehicle steers.

Leather gloves cover my fists, and I challenge you to defy my friend.
Let integrity standing tall be the message we will send.

You Cheated Me

You lost the race with life and are now dead.
I was cheated, my love, when this world you fled.

Your cleverness has outfoxed me again.
I lost the dash to die first, much to my chagrin.

Your management of everything is now gone.
An abrupt change for me as I meet the dawn.

For years my dear, we have joked about this time.
I miss you, my girl. To heaven, I will climb.

Cautiously Pick Your Words

The remark is caustic, in your opinion, you state.
Her feelings were shattered, but you did not hesitate.

Some words are treacherous and cut like a sharp blade.
You can't retract them; the damage has been made.

Cautiously pick your words, my child; some fears may choose your fate.
With back to the wall, soft and tender might win a debate.

A whisper from a baby's lips can champion a fool's shouts.
And wisdom from special words can satisfy our own doubts.

Shadows of Life

The shadows of life sometimes consume the gems that hide in the corners.
The realities of the hereafter are concealed from the mourners.

Minuscule secrets silently float around in the atmosphere.
A maize of emotional waves can cause or dry a lonely tear.

May we mend a broken heart with the complexities of remarks we make.
Let the hidden gems from our ancestors merge to bring us awake.

Phone Panic

I can't find my cell phone, and I'm starting to get panicky.
My world has stopped as I've lost my lifeline to humanity.

My blood pressure is rising, and my pulse is erratic.
I am trying to stay calm and not be so dramatic.

This phone has become part of my body, frightening as it can be.
Without it, this cloudy brain ceases to function. Don't you see?

I know my girlfriend is texting me. What can I possibly do?
A dental appointment I thought was tomorrow. But is it true?

My life is disintegrating. I have nowhere to turn.
Oh, to hear that familiar ring, and for it, I yearn.

I've looked in my coat pockets and in the car, as well.
I drove to my friend's house and checked with other personnel.

I'm not talking on it or holding it, which is sometimes the case.
It's not at any of my three charging stations; I've checked each place.

No, not under my car seat or caught in the crack by the console.
I must locate this runaway today. It will be my goal.

Those ubiquitous cell phones saturate the planet, but where is mine?
The dreaded answer is that I must order a new one online!

Fourteen hundred dollars. Are you kidding me, my friend?
I'll have to take a loan because there is no money I can spend.

World Cruise 2023 Island Princess

If a cruise ship I board that encircles the earth,
From Los Angeles to Australia with a stop in Perth.

This packing is a challenge. How many shirts do I take?
It's a four-month cruise, and my weakness is carrot cake.

How much cash do I need, foreign currency for sure?
My pickpocket pants will keep my money secure.

From LA to Hawaii is often a rough ride.
A seasick pill can help your tummy turn the tide.

Fellow passengers I greet, this cruise will be fun.
Let's meet on the top deck and soak up some sun.

The nightly entertainment is among the very best.
After a show and a drink, go to your room and rest.

At our equator crossing, the doldrums we may find.
The ocean can be a sea of glass, bringing peace to your mind.

The Panama and the Suez so different they are.
No locks have the Suez; we'll discuss this in the bar.

Singapore, Sri Lanka, and Dubai, we will soon see.
Malta, Casablanca, and Barcelona, we do agree.

The tranquil Pacific Ocean is only sometimes at ease.
Enjoy the beauty of her waves; take a picture if you please.

Seven days to cross the Atlantic, might a bird fly by?
What destination lies ahead? Just check your Wi-Fi.

The cruise ends soon, but I don't want to go home.
The oceans of the world, I'll continue to roam.

Prolong My Years

It is radioactive and is meant to prolong my years.
The thought of healing electron beams invading my body calms my fears.

Ironically, I was born in July, and my Zodiac sign is Cancer.
Can my treatment be effective? Only God will know the answer.

I do not fear death. It is part of living our last fleeting moment.
Might we meet with dignity the experience of heaven's enrollment?

Slow down. I probably have years yet to live until this disease seals my fate.
May the wonders of science and medicine solve this problem with my prostate.

Help

She rubbed blood on her body from a dead friend.
Nineteen lifeless children, we can't comprehend.

We're in trouble; we're in trouble, nine-one-one!
America cries out; they were shot with a gun.

Words from an eleven-year-old pierce my head.
All the people that she knew now were dead.

Two beautiful dedicated teachers,
Their lovely pictures show smiling facial features.

Our hearts and minds scream for a solution.
Ideas abound with disagreement pollution.

Twenty years in the future, will it be the same?
All directions, the fingers point, and who's to blame?

Tranquility

The tranquility of the cloud is violently erased when sharp spikes jut out.
The sun sneaks silently around the edges of the whiteness, exposing its own clout.

Our peers' eyelashes shutter as each sunbeam pierce their existence.
And we sheepishly gaze at each other, contemplating what will happen hence.

The white cloud regains its composure and returns to its soft pale fluffiness of peace.
But the pangs of war and the nearness of death will not retreat, nor will they cease.

And the equator races at 1,000 miles per hour, yet the poles stand still.
Let's pledge our souls to the good side and bless our children with integrity. I will!

The Drifter

He's a drifter with no family to claim.
His life's in shambles, with only him to blame.

He was raised in an orphanage and was too old to adopt.
Chopping wood and bussing dishes, his confidence has dropped.

She works at this restaurant bussing with him.
The lady lives in Texas; we think her name is Kim.

A single mother with five kids from six to eighteen.
No help from the father, and his presence is unseen.

The drifter could use a friend, and they're both down and out.
A smile at her creates a spark, without a doubt.

She thinks no man would want her with five kids to attend.
But now, a wink comes through, a message he does send.

The middle-aged lady's pulse starts to feel funny.
Her heart is acting like a soft, cuddled bunny.

Two human beings have been looking for an answer.
The drifter likes this lady and wants to romance her.

Five children to take care of is an ominous task.
He would marry her, but he's too nervous to ask.

His old car is a pile of junk, embarrassing to show.
Her car is much nicer; a date they can go.

The confidence that infatuation can create.
He touches her hand, and she responds. It is fate.

She owns her house, and maybe her sister will assist them.
Kim's sure the kids will help and think they won't condemn him.

The drifter is astonished; the plans are moving fast.
He's yet to propose to her; will this marriage last?

The restaurant owner loans the drifter the money.
An emerald-cut diamond he buys for his honey.

The cooks, dishwashers, and servers are in the wedding.
The drifter and his girl on a honeymoon they're heading.

Our Little Ones

We honor you, our little ones. You are the phoenix of the earth.
Encouragement we bestow on you. May your existence be flooded in mirth.

Collect new goals and create adventurous thoughts as you undertake the journey of life.
Persevere through the detriments of living and fight off the pangs of strife.

Immerse yourself with supportive companions and motivate your inner being.
Stand up and remain strong, warding off threats as you watch your opponent's fleeing.

Cautiously make left turns in your daily actions. Their surprise endings are dangerous.
Addictions are disguised in every form. Temptations are free and generous.

Stand tall for your family and friends. Cover them with a protective blanket.
May the children of the world mature to be guardians of this spinning planet.

A Sad Puppy

It started as a typical day with dogs in the park.
They wagged their tails, blinked their eyes, and all liked to bark.

But one puppy was all alone, standing to the side.
Tears rolled down her cheeks, and she thought of suicide.

A large collie observed this situation.
He winked at the puppy, thinking a friendship would be fun.

The puppy's tail wagged twice, and a smile formed on her face.
The collie was eager to have a friend to embrace.

All the other dogs took note of the collie's friend.
They howled and barked, and the welcome mat they did extend.

Senior Dancing

If a dance, I would do that would pertain to you and me.
Is it East Coast or West Coast, but fun, don't you agree?

Oh my, dear lady, much older I am than you.
You are a high stepper with your red high heel shoe.

A Stetson I'm wearing, but a cowboy I'm not.
My boots, mam, with pointed toes, yesterday I bought.

Have you married my lass? Your paisley blouse is nice.
Also, do you gamble? With me, we could roll the dice.

It's polka now. With a new partner, I will dance.
She asks, "Can we spin instead of a backward prance?"

"Of course, my new friend. We will spin counterclockwise."
This dance ended. It was sad when we said our goodbyes.

We admire that couple doing the West Coast swing.
They've dressed so attractively and look at their bling.

Her beads are colorful, and her earrings dangle.
As she dances with her bow, it appears they tangle.

Your belt buckle, sir is impressive indeed.
I want to buy one now that you have taken the lead.

It's Cha Cha now, ask a partner and learn this rhythm.
I'm learning this step and building my dance wisdom.

It's country, triple step, walk, walk, teach this to me.
I love these senior dances; learning is free.

Three nights a week and live bands are performing.
Swing, waltz, fox trot, country, "These boots are made for walking!"

Slinging Whiskey

She's a whiskey slinger at a busy local bar.
Her first husband left, and now the second; it's so bizarre.
Twenty-three years of bartending, an exciting career,
The drunks all love her as she runs to serve them beer.

It's psychiatry at work; Molly gives them hope.
Problems are solved, and advice is quoted from the pope.
Sure, Molly drinks a little; she needs to give sound advice.
Professional help is expensive; Molly's is half-price.

Molly and the tequila saved old Bill's life.
The man's contagious drunken smile brought back his lovely wife.
Sometimes the boisterous image of the drink,
Is magnified by Carrie Nation and brought to the brink.

It has slowed the business at Molly's famous bar.
She must sell her Golden Noodle and her luxury car.
But the die-hard drunks that love their pleasant life,
Will increase Molly's tips and decrease her strife.

A whiskey slinger must sometimes be the bouncer.
Some patrons throw chairs, as shown by a TV announcer.
Molly uses John Wayne toilet paper, and she is tough.
The words spoken in this bar are sometimes naughty and rough.

And when a biker arrives and revs up his Harley,
Prepare for a song on Touch Tunes, sung by Bob Marley.
The tavern has a small dance floor; they like the east-coast swing.
The drinkers tap their feet when Molly plays Elvis the King.

The pool tables are fine, and the competition is hot.
A vodka-laden smarty pants makes a three-rail bank shot.
Shuffleboard is a precision game played with several pucks.
This game plays for money; in a row, line up your ducks.

When the day is done, a city unwinds in its bars.
Nerves are settled, friends are made, and we all shoot for the stars.

The Stalker

This poem is 100% fiction and meant to diversify my genre to make a future book more interesting. I started the idea after watching a lady's makeup commercial featuring her eyes. No, I am not being stalked, LOL!

Her eyes are shocking by an electric show.
The pupils are magnified by an eerie glow.

Her piercing look invades my privacy.
From the clutches of her grasp, I must flee.

Memories from the past are haunting my mind.
These violent thoughts, I must keep confined.

My feelings intensify as the day ends.
With her stalking behavior, a text she sends.

There's no escaping my devotion to you.
Our relationship must begin anew.

The Little Kangaroo

He cannot learn to hop, the little kangaroo.
Even with extensive training, this is still true.

So, embarrassing it is, his girlfriend can hop.
She can spin in circles and do the bop.

In the early days, her boyfriend's foot was burned.
The elders of the community were quite concerned.

The local surgeons are puzzled at best.
But a new doctor attacks the problem with zest.

The three-hour surgery was a total success.
A bionic foot is attached, oh yes.

And now this couple can hop together.
They just know their love will last forever!

Inebriated

I'm an alcoholic. Will you drink with me?
Release me from this guilt, and set me free.

I've tried to quit, and I aim to cut down.
But the morning mirror greets me with a frown.

Crown is good, vodka too, tequila, oh my.
AA's suggestions, I do defy.

I try to wait till five o'clock to drink.
But often, by two, I'm on the brink.

Noticing lately that I might start by ten.
I used to skip a day, but I can't remember when.

Thank you, my friend, for this hobby we share.
Let's face the truth. It's our lifetime affair.

Pulchritudinous

Your beauty, my dear, people recognize.
If blue ribbons are given, you will win the prize.

Although attractive is sometimes a curse,
Not having it is often worse.

Your attire, my lady, is way at the top.
You are graded on this subject by the fashion cop.

Jewelry, of course, you like silver or gold.
When it comes to elegance, you break the mold.

You accept my date, so I stop to rejoice.
I'll be your escort to the place of your choice!

Jungle Giraffe

The giraffe's neck is the talk of the town.
His head is so high that he always looks down.

The creatures hold him in the highest esteem.
His friends are many, and so it does seem.

A menagerie reveres his loyalty.
He protects the creatures below he can see.

As the old giraffe ages, his eyes begin to dim.
Who can oversee the jungle for him?

Grandfather, I want to take over for you.
Yes, Grandson, an occupation you must pursue.

You will warn fellow friends when danger does lurk.
Follow my legacy of diligence as you work!

Mouse & Cat

The mouse imagines the cat as a nuisance.
A Calico Cat thinks the mouse is a dunce.

Her colorful attire is showy, indeed.
With her nose in the air, a sarcastic breed.

Although raised in the church, the mouse is not nice.
He's clever and smart, and his plans are precise.

Unaware of what the mouse has up his sleeve,
Miss Calico, nonchalantly, the church she does leave.

With the snooty girl gone, he puts bugs in her bed.
The morning headlines read the mouse is found dead!

1870 Cowboy

His hands are callused, and his face leathered.
This calf he ropes is still and tethered.

The stench from the branding iron is unpleasant.
Memories from this cowboy's past are present.

Strapped to his side is a ten-inch Bowie knife.
A weapon he needs as he rides through life.

From Texas to Abilene, the longhorns they are.
Months in the saddle, his journey looms far.

A 45-caliber Colt is his best friend.
This gun has introduced six to their end.

The horse sees it first, a Diamondback Rattlesnake.
Bang!.... In the sun, this reptile's body will bake.

His gunfighter reflexes are instant.
Experience teaches him to be vigilant.

This year brings a half million cattle to Abilene.
The rain is dancing, and the prairie shows off her green.

Beneath the cowboy gallops a spirited Pinto.
The moisture accents Oklahoma with a rainbow.

They ford the Cimarron River with three thousand head.
The river is running high, and forty-five cattle are dead.

The men are exhausted and covet a break.
Whiskey they need and a glass they will take.

Smoke fills the Oklahoma Tavern as each buys a drink.
The cowboy sees her behind the bar; her blouse is pink.

Other men notice this lady, and one insults her.
The cowboy cuts this man by kicking him with his spur.

1870 Cowboy

The liquor enhances the violence, and all hell breaks loose.
The fists fly, and the jaws are broken; It is total abuse.

The cowboy manages to talk to the barmaid.
She feels safe with him and no longer afraid.

He buys her a drink, and they sit at the bar.
The lady likes this unshaven face that hides an ugly scar.

She softly touches his shoulder and looks him in the face.
Take me with you. I need to get out of this place.

The whiskey softens his mood, but he knows she can't go.
It's too dangerous for a woman; he must ride solo.

Suddenly he hears his name, "Josh, get the men ready.
It's raining, and this is a twister country. Hold the herd steady."

"Will do, Boss." Tom, Norm, and Jake take the west side of the herd."
The tornado appears instantly. Josh's vision is blurred.

He is separated from his Pinto and is slammed to the ground.
He thinks of the barmaid and hopes she is Abilene bound.

Morning finds three men dead, including the owner, Boss.
Two hundred cattle dead is a significant financial loss.

Josh, who is second in command, now takes over the reins.
In three days, most of the strays are gathered from the plains.

Josh yells, "We'll, take the herd through Wichita and pick up more men.
Tom, you stock the chuck wagon. Our supplies are running thin."

Two days out of Wichita, a stranger rides into view.
With two pistols on his hips, he spits out his chew.

His demeanor is cocky, "Got any grub? I can't wait."
Josh suspiciously tells the cook, "Give the man a plate."

1870 Cowboy

Dusk is approaching as everyone watches the herd.
The gunfighter, patch on one eye, eats and never says a word.

Suddenly both guns are pointed at Josh by the intruder.
I want your cash box, and don't challenge me as a shooter.

Josh knew any gunfire might stampede the cattle.
The cook drops a roasting pan, and this creates a rattle.

In a split second, Josh's Bowie Knife flies through the air.
Piercing the gunslinger's heart, he doesn't stand a prayer.

Daybreak finds the cattle drive heading north again.
A new hand joined them in Wichita. His nickname is Ben.

Ben is pretty handy with a gun, and rustlers are about.
He worked for the army as a skilled and dedicated scout.

Josh is lonely, and his thoughts dwell on the Oklahoma barmaid.
He'll find her on the way back, and with his guitar, he will serenade.

It's getting dark, and shots ring out from the herd's west side.
Josh yells at Ben, "Shoot some rustlers.!" "Will do!" Ben replies.

Josh has ten cowboys, many of whom are skilled with a gun.
The cattle thieves are liquored up, and the fight has just begun.

Tom says, "The courage that liquor gives them will cost each their life.
Josh and his men hang three of the rustlers. What a day of strife.

Jake and Norm are shot, and the cook gives them whiskey for pain.
Norm isn't wounded but wants to know where there's whiskey he can obtain.

Abilene is a week away. The deceased Boss's wife owns the herd.
The boss promised Josh thirty percent of the profit. This was his word.

The men are getting restless as the final days are ending.
They start to think about the money they will soon be spending.

1870 Cowboy

The Longhorns are in holding pens after being driven into town.
The cattle buyers are anxious to put their money down.

Josh and the herd owner, Ma'am Ellie, will get a ton of cash.
All the cowboys get their pay and off to the Saloon they dash.

The cattle are loaded on rail cars, and off to Chicago, they go.
Josh follows the men to the Saloon, hoping to see a show.

He sits at the bar. The music is loud, and smoke fills the room.
The girl who is singing on stage wears a lavish gold costume.

"Would you like to buy me a drink, stranger?" came the voice.
Josh turned around, and there she was. It was time to rejoice!

The girl he met in Oklahoma was now here in Abilene.
"Now I know your name is Maddy, and you are my cowgirl queen."

"Nice to meet you again, Josh. I was hoping to see you here.
Sit at a table. I'll grab a drink, and you say you want a beer?"

"Maddy, I'm not getting any younger and want to buy my own place.
I need a mate to help me start a new life. I'll dress you in lace."

"Josh, I wanted you from the first instant we met. We'll be a team.
I would love to be with you and help follow your dream."

Depression

As the morning abruptly plunges into the girl's private domain, the tiny spasms of light ricochet off the beveled square mirror above her dresser, hitting the disobedient eyelids that refuse to meet the punishment of the day. Her body defiantly jerks as her tiny trembling fingers clinch the handmade quilt and pull it over her head, then roll to her tummy, bend her knees to a fetal position, and squeeze a second pillow tight against her inner thighs.

This seventeen-year-old beauty fights pangs of misery, and she fears sliding into the black hole repeatedly, unable to escape to only one thought of authentic happiness. Sally squeezes her eyelids tighter, desperately inventing new defense mechanisms to fight her deep depression. She is losing the battle, and the first tear leaks between the black eyelashes then wet this perfect, smoothly textured cheek before landing on a crinkled silk pillowcase. The first feeling of moisture opens the floodgates, and the precious child literally sobs her heart out, gasping for each breath of air between screams of pain.

A tiny calico kitty is trapped under the covers, then escapes and affectionately licks Sally's cheek. The small rough sandpaper tongue slowly drags across the unwrinkled skin again and again and now again. Sally's screams cease, and her uncontrolled sobbing slows to a whimpering sound, not unlike a small child begging for sympathy and love.

The seventeen-year-olds swollen eyelids fight to display pupils that sadly but curiously gaze at the kitten through blurred, teary blue eyes. She cuddles this tiny friend against her shallow cleavage and feels the warmness and love transferring into her rapidly beating heart. The thoughts of depression dissipate for a few seconds before the dread reoccurs, spreading to another day of gloom.

Depression

Sally's parents support her in every way possible, with highly reputable psychiatrists and the latest expensive medicine. This unwanted affliction does not plague their other two children.

Sally's mom, Jan, softly asked, "Are you ready for breakfast, maybe an over-easy egg and piece of crisp bacon or a bowl of sugar-coated Cheerios?"

Sally forces a weak smile on her loving mother and responds, "Cereal will be fine, mom, thank you." She continues to hold the small puff of the multi-colored calico kitty fur firmly against her body. This newly acquired bit of a friend might be the start of a building block to a possibly better sunshine day.

"Mom, has Bill called? I still don't have a date for the junior-senior prom, and this is my next to the last year."

"No, honey, I'm sorry. There's still plenty of time."

Sally fantasizes - - - even if the brilliant nerd Jack asked me, I would go. He is different, for sure, but he can dance. His car is embarrassing. Maybe he could take his dad's? I want Bill, but so do Susie and Jennifer and every other girl in school.

For a few minutes, she had forgotten about her depression as she was boy-dreaming. Her nerd friend Jack also has signs of mild depression, and they often talk about it. Talking to anyone about it helps. You don't need a hundred-dollar-an-hour psychiatrist always to be the person listening.

The small kitty against Sally's chest has its motor running, which cushions the anxiety this seventeen-year-old has captured within her.

The psychiatrist has started Sally on a new anti-depressant medicine, and at times she thinks it is helping.

Depression

"Mom, come quick and look out the window!"

The nerd with cute red hair and thick glasses just pulled up to the curb in that embarrassing contraption he drives. He exits the car on the street side and, after skipping around the front of the car, walks up to Sally's door and rings the doorbell.

She opens the door with, "Jack! Hello. What's going on?"

Jack sheepishly mumbles, "I have a new puppy and thought you might like to come over and see him. He's not registered or anything special. I guess he's a Heinz 57."

"Of course, I'd love to go. Let me get a jacket. I'd better leave my kitten here. This raggedy old denim coat will be perfect for playing with a rowdy puppy."

Sally's heart fluttered as she excitedly entered the car after Jack finally got the broken handle to open the door. The ride was amazingly comfortable in this outdated full-sized four-door green Chrysler sedan. The paint on the hood was almost wholly weathered away. They looked at each other and laughed. Jack's house was soon in view with a barking canine looking to be half Husky and part German Shepherd sticking his moist nose through the picket fence.

"He's beautiful," blurts out Sally. "Where did you get him?"

"The neighbors up the road were giving puppies away, so I took one. He's exciting to play with."

Sally immediately hugged this furry bundle of joy and rolled in the grass with him. The dog grabbed her coat sleeve and started a tug of war.

Depression

Jack joined enthusiastically and pulled the puppy away from Sally's coat. In thirty minutes, all three were exhausted and lay on the thick green lawn.

As all three-lay side by side, Jack said, "We've had many talks, Sally, about our depression through the years. I want to thank you for being my friend and sounding board sincerely. The ones who aren't depressed don't have a clue, and the ones who are depressed understand it completely. No matter which direction our lives go, we can always call or text each other if we need a pep talk."

Jack leaned over and kissed her on the lips. Sally was happy this old friendship had been rekindled. She held his hand as they walked to the car.

Back at Sally's house, he walked her to the door. "By the way, Sally, is there any way you would go to the prom with me?"

To the County Line

I love you to the county line and back.
It is a fur piece, my lady. We should take a snack.

Your beauty as we go enhances my praise for you.
This road is time-consuming and bumpy too.

The grass is tall, and small rodents scurry about.
We'll be there, honey, in time, without a doubt.

I've been so nervous to say, but I love you, Myrtle.
I love you too, my handsome young man, the Turtle.

Constipated

I'm so constipated that I will never eat cheese again.
Don't take this distorted face as a sheepish grin.

It all started when we went to that party yesterday.
Assorted cheeses were on everything, I must say.

There was blue cheese, cheddar, smoked gouda, and Velveeta.
I packed in the food and then a margarita.

Morning finds me in an unpleasant predicament.
It appears treatment with medicine is imminent!

I'm starting with that powder that you mix with water.
No more parties for me until I'm feeling much better.

Mr. Tall Skyscraper

Mr. Tall Skyscraper looks down from his lofty perch and observes the small human specs below.
Confused miniature yellow cabs drive manically in all directions challenging the men in blue.

Mr. Tall sees the human specs rushing into his building to start their busy day.
Thousands will ride the elevators and go to their own small cubicle to stay.

Humanity in all shapes and forms is changing the way this city thinks.
Let these young minds rescue us before our endangered Titanic sinks.

Will the new kid on the block (artificial intelligence) heal our injury?
Or will he trick us with clouds and hard drives full of perjury?

Silence

It was unusual at the time. The silence would not whisper.
The pandemonium ceased as if it came from scripture.

Calmed emotions listened to the nothings in the air.
Having no conception of the meaning of this peaceful silent care.

Let a gentle music entry bathe our pores and soothe our nerves.
May the road ahead be straight and absent of dangerouse curves.

The Streets are not Paved with Gold

It's a little town, and the streets are not paved in gold.
The small children mostly do as they are told.

This is rural America, folks, a great place to hang out.
The main drug here is Tylenol, without a doubt.

All the dogs have their favorite fire hydrant here in town.
Give a smile to everyone, as if they wear a crown.

The difference between this place and a big city is profound.
Traffic here hasn't been invented yet, just ask around.

If you meet a car or pick-up truck, the driver will wave.
Waving is safer than texting. It's all the rage.

The rumor is that middle America is a bellwether.
It's the glue that hold the edges of this country together.

Tragedy

The siren is screaming as the ambulance flies by.
A mother's tears have stopped, and her cheeks are now dry.

From the clutches of steel, the jaws of life have freed her child.
She and the paramedics ride with her son. The drive is wild.

The precious four-year-old has two compound fractured legs.
With tear-soaked cheeks and quivering lips, for sympathy, he begs.

They are broadsided at an intersection on a foggy night.
The ambulance spins, and the boy from his gurney takes flight.

His legs are not protected as he collides with the floor.
His mother's courage is shattered, and she is slammed against the door.

Instantly police cars arrive at this intersection.
Traffic is jammed with cars moving in every direction.

The paramedics, although covered in blood, take action.
EMS starts an emergency chain reaction.

An ambulance with flashing lights soon arrives on the scene.
The boy is loaded into the ambulance. His pain is extreme.

The man that T-boned them is dead. He smells of alcohol.
After loading the patients, the driver creeps through the fog at a crawl.

The traffic is fierce, and the siren is wailing as they drive.
A cell phone rings, and now the father's voice, "Is my son still alive?"

The mother, although still in shock, responds. "Yes, honey, he is!"
The tears flood the face of this lady that the precious boy calls his.

A Brief Thought - Friendship

*I had no idea where this thought was heading
when it was started. I love the last line.*

Olga Trushina

A Brief Thought – Friendship

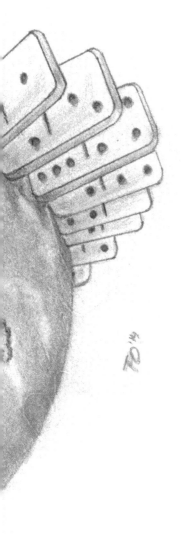

A friendship originates in a flash of thought, an impulse of brain waves, a minute whisper of intelligent imagination. It's birth at zero, it builds from a grain of sand, composing the pieces as the crescendo grows. Increasing, intensifying from byte to megabytes, the power accumulates and concentrates on the subject in a caring, loving manner, and is caused by an unselfish attitude that is nourished by a look, a smile, or a twinkling eye. It can happen in an instant and be cultivated for a lifetime. It affects all ages and is immensely contagious, spreading from person to person, continent to continent like falling dominoes, in multicolors. Whether it comes in the name of friendship, peace or love, it is spoken in a multitude of languages and is a possession held by all classes of people. It is a powerful source of energy, impossible to measure with scientific instruments, and is tugging on the human race like the moon pulls on planet earth. The future chapters and those since the birth of man are written on the faces surrounding us.

First Impression

The wrinkled and weathered skin does not hide his personality or friendships.
The black square patch on his left eye does not cover the smile on his lips.

Nor does the black patch mask the twinkle in the old man's other eye.
This high mileage body conceals the triumphs of youth gone by.

Imprisoned by nostalgia, the old man's psyche begs for new avenues.
Not to relive yesteryear but break out with mesmerizing, captivating news.

Let a peek at tomorrow create new thoughts and vibrant inventions.
May our cerebral capacity stretch to absorb these comprehensions.